Pulse

Vino x Anntidote

When messy mortals merge
to take a chance on their dreams
they birth a kaleidoscope of moments.

Love

Look at me

Love is so easy

Loss

I miss you

Its unfair

Finding yourself

FPP

My hair

Acceptance

Im single

I stink

Moving on

Dont listen

See for yourself

Chapter 1: Love

Intro

The longing for Love lingers in the living
an impulse to initiate intimacy because
we crave to console creatures that captivate our compassion
spurring us to stride into strange schemes to satisfy this lurid addiction
a union of the flesh, mind, soul – an obsessive thirst for a deeper union
with one's self or with another being bound to breathe the same fate
as we cross the treacherous rapids that test our worth
we're born into an understanding of what it is to be human
we worship those who've waged war and won in the name of Love
saints whose names are sanctified in songs and scripts as symbols
of sweet salvation that awaits those who strive
to be embraced in the warmth of another's heart
so we stand and salute in solemn vow to seek the same sensation.

Look at me

I am a writer, and with each movement of my hand I am caressing the walls of
my soul to see where the cracks are and which pieces are coming loose
I let the tip of my pen glide through the darkness to make way for the light
So you can see into the black that has tainted the colour spectrum of my mind
With each new word I chisel away at my heart
And the dust that falls is what I present to you
This blank page is filled with nothing more than screams morphed into ink
This image I'm painting in your mind's eye is nothing more than a rippled
reflection of what sleeps behind mine; the emotions I invoke are nothing more
than wishes of my feelings, which are broken
To be healed through an understanding of your perception of my twisted reality
What I present to you isn't words or sentences; it's not even a poem
It's comfort for when pain finds you and you feel alone; know that I'm there too
It's an outline for the way back when darkness has dragged you in too deep
Grab a hold of my sentences to find your way back
Use my syllables to nourish yourself when life has taken everything you need
When you hear the steps of depression creep in your hallway
Use my life as an alarm to scare him away
Let my creativity show you what my voice is unable to tell you
Invite all the words in this piece and throw a farewell party for sadness
I want – no, I need to help you
If my art isn't making the world better, I don't deserve the title of poet
If you can't relate to my pieces, I can't don the name author
If you can't see me in what I write, I have failed as a writer
My life is the frame
My love is the canvas
My soul is the ink
My heart is the brush
My pain is the inspiration
My everything is the result
I give myself to you through my art

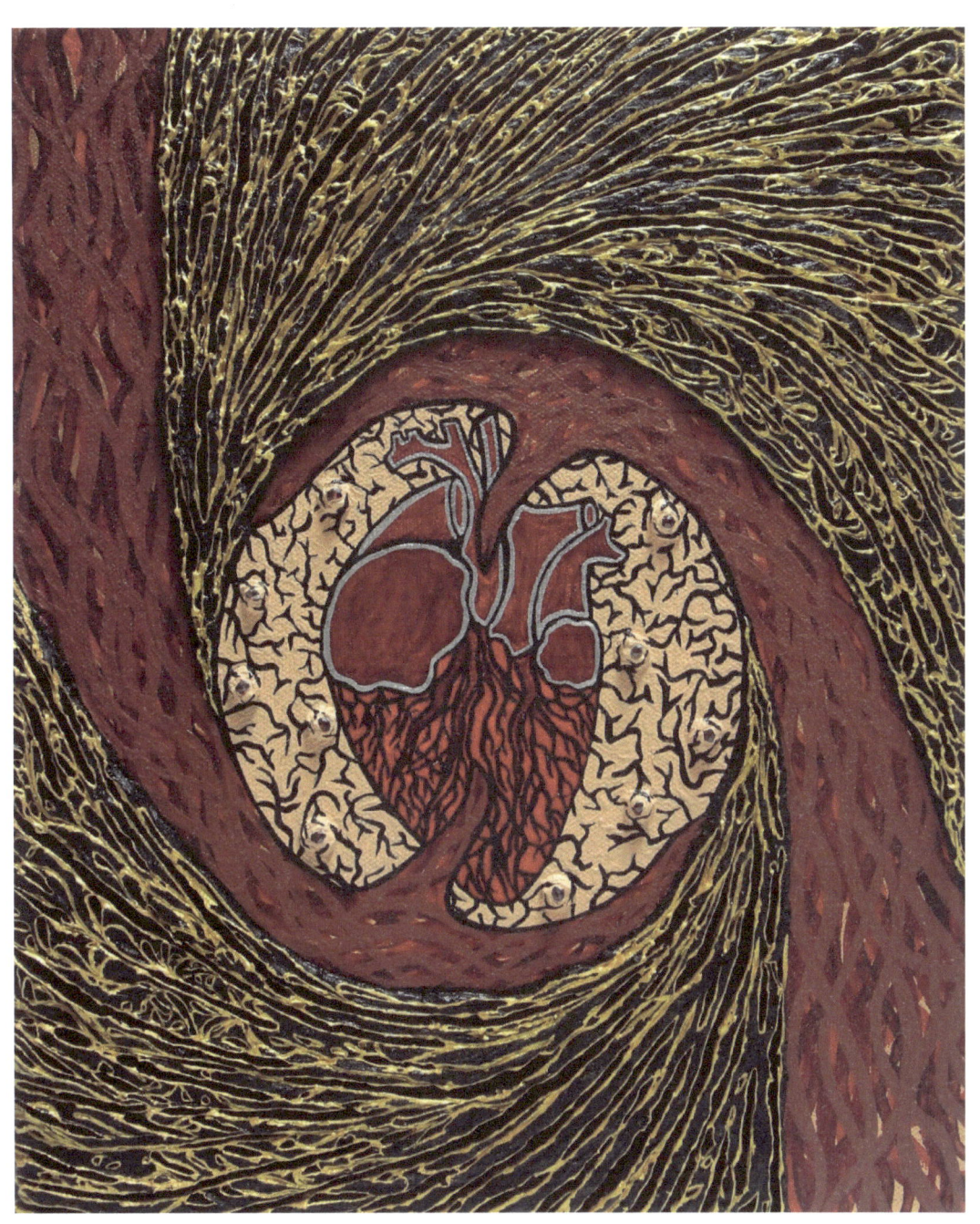

Love is so easy

If you have nothing, I will give you everything
If the sky won't let up with the tears it drops, let me cover you
When the waves of regret are close to drowning you, take my hand
When the sun is taking too long to come up, let me write you some light
If the darkness refuses to let go of you, let my heart convince him
If the pain is about to break you, let my soul heal everything
Take me when you feel you don't have enough
Use my hands when you can't find the edges of hope
Use my lungs if despair has filled yours with smoke
Let my love hug you when you're cold
Let my words counter the lies that are told
If everyone tells you "You can't do it", let's work together to prove them wrong
If there is no one in your corner,
let me show you that my shoulder is eternally strong
If black and white are spinning too fast,
let me be the centre that holds it together
When your fever is running amok, let me kiss you till you feel better
I just want to show you that it can be real
I want to know what it feels like to "feel"
Let me write poems that will articulate feelings that have been neglected
Let me paint a story with words so pure the paint itself will tell you I meant it
Make life feel guilty for not living up to its promise
And let "us" be the beginning of a never-ending story
Let our love carry us into eternity and intertwine with the lost pages of history
Let our love be the greatest yet and have our story leave a legacy

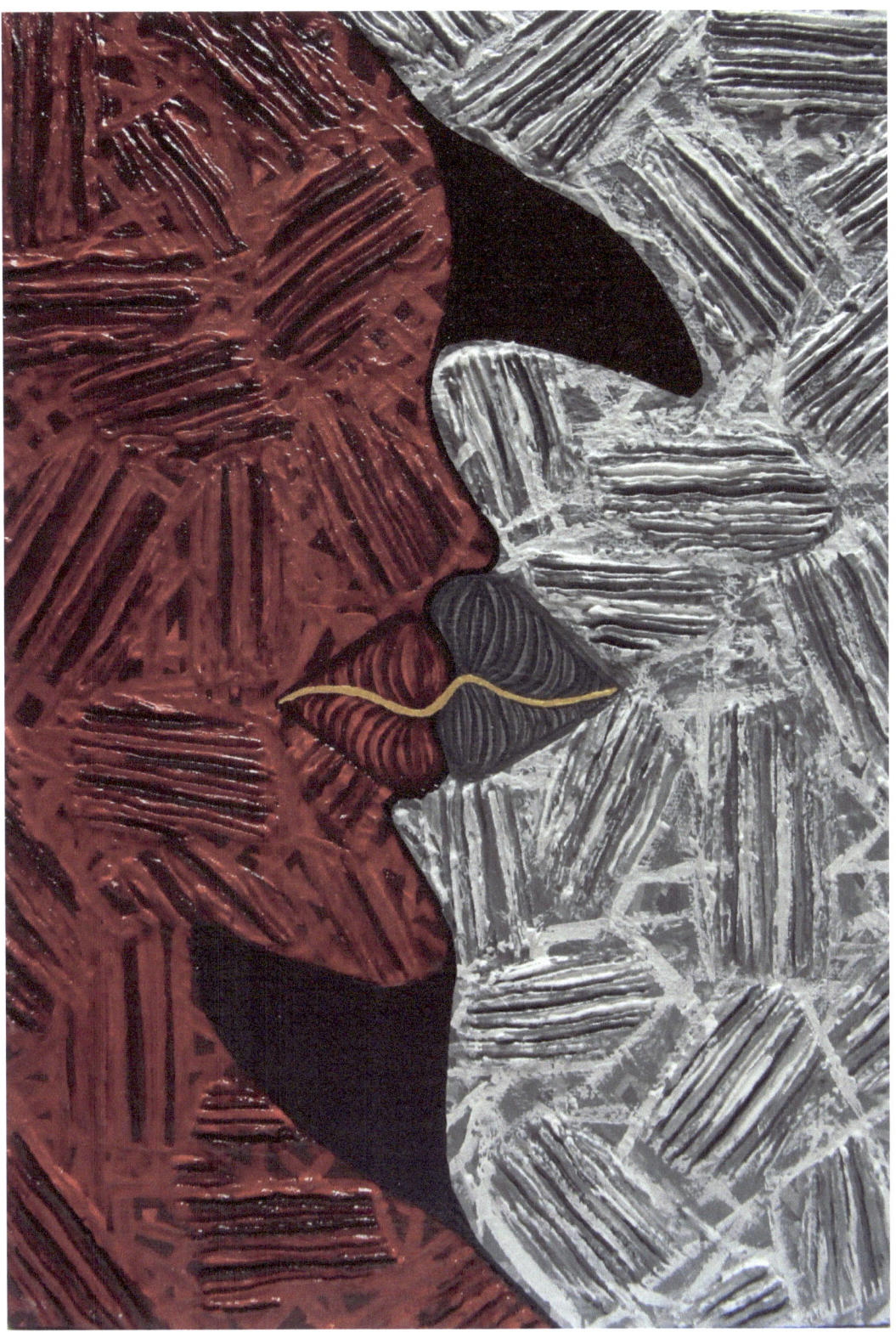

Outro

As some slumber on vanity's sand
we stay awake wondering
the ways in which we may set in motion
the world's pulse that beats for significance
whom will we change for if not for us
who will we love if not one another
who will live on if we are
left with nothing
live with nothing
and leave with nothing
it's futile to forage in an infertile field for it feeds no one
sacrifice is needed to sow seeds in service to the cause
yet few fork the fees into the earth, so Love laments for the living
as famine starves the many souls left lonely
while its fruits rot away in seclusion.

Chapter 2: Loss

Intro

You unstitched the tendons that held my heart whole
to marinate in the juices of my love
yet you didn't prepare your soul
for the darkness of my depths
the ride through my flaws proved too much
the experience plundered your purpose at pride's pit stop
you abandoned me with my gaping wounds
they unravelled; only for your eyes, but now everyone sees
I waste away in the swamp of stale memories
where we once bathed to be born anew
now I brace myself to drown in
another body to be buried beneath the ivory banner
of broken hearts festering in surrender
this is why the depth of one's heart must remain a mystery.

I miss you

There is this letter on my nightstand I wrote for you
And placing it on yours is something I've been trying to do
But there are these hidden lines I dare not cross
Laid down by customs where pride is the boss
And shame its henchmen, restricting my so-called "wants"
I have this notebook in the pocket of my favourite pants
I filled each page with poems about you
I've been hinting at it for weeks now, every day I've been giving you a clue
But to reach deep down and take it out terrifies me
For after that, I would have to place it in your hand
Just imagining you keeping your hands in your pockets is too scary
I have this ideal setup in mind for when, but things never go as planned
I have this text in my phone I wrote while you were away
I've been wanting to divide it into pieces and send you one a day
But my bars are never sufficient to send it
My service keeps telling me it's too long, I have to shorten it
But whenever I open it, I inexplicably keep adding to it
Someday I will trade phones with you, so you can read it as it is
And understand what love is
I have this Word document in my cloud I can't seem to share
It has over a million variations of the question "Do you still care?"
Whenever I want to link you to it, I get this pop-up telling me I can't do it
Because the file has been corrupted, but for some reason I can still write in it
I have this one word written on the palm of my hand
I want to caress your cheek and see if it will stay with you
I can't wash my hands, can't shake hands, can't even wave anymore
Not until I give it to you
I have these Post-its that I wrote
Because all my regular paper became too soggy
I now have a closet full of yellow, green, blue
and grey notes to make you happy
At least I think they will make you happy
Because who wouldn't want to be missed like this?
They told me my heart wouldn't be able to handle a love this true
I already know that you miss me less than I miss you
I already know that you've moved on
I know these feelings to be wrong
But that doesn't prevent me from crying
That doesn't prevent me from writing
I have these words for you
And one day I will give them to you

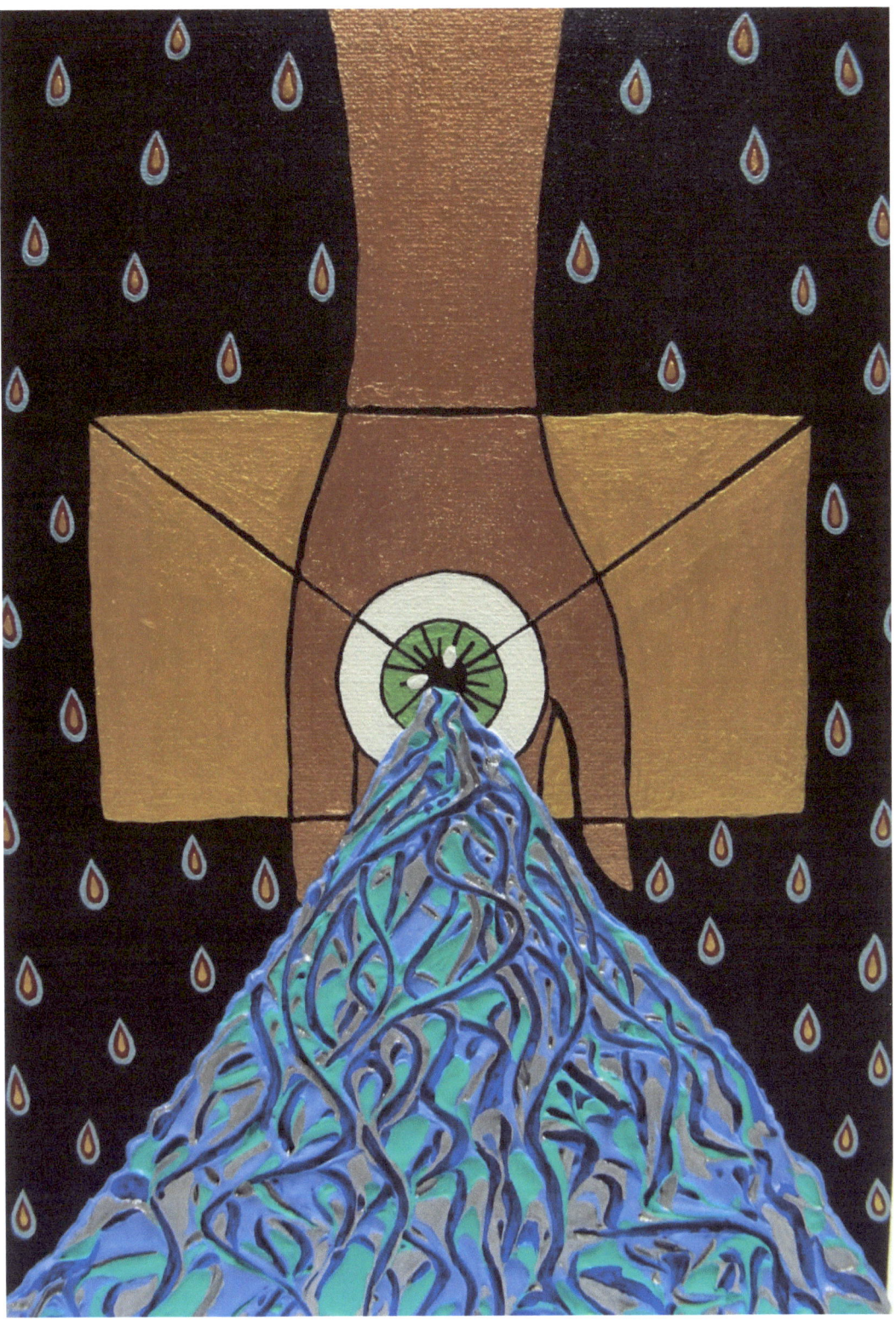

Its unfair

Sometimes I still read your words,
as if I want to remind myself I need to miss you
Compare each line to mine to see if I measure up to you
In my mind I visit the beach you wrote about
and watch the waves crash near my feet
I reread each sentence and gaze at the space in between,
hoping the emptiness will speak
You were the other side of my inner writer whom I never knew was missing
I know a reply isn't coming to my last message but foolishly I'm still waiting
Hoping that perhaps a rift in time will allow you to tell me you're okay
When I lost you, you took away everything beautiful a poet could say
Now I'm merely tracing words written by a shell of emotions I can't feel
Writing along the edges of acceptance and each line ends with "Is this real?"
The tears that fell when I heard you'd jumped still stain my heart
The friendship I lost took my happiness and ripped it apart
I taped it together with the Band-Aids depression gave me
Guess what? Even he was crying; seems without you even he feels lonely
The similarities we had put us on the same road of life
I had to put my pen to the side and use a pencil to talk to life
Because certainty of survival or maintaining was lost
Hope got dragged into the dark, screaming and kicking, but it was for naught
I want to practise every religion known to man and go through every rite
Just so I can ask every God out there to give me another moment with you
I don't miss you because I love you
I miss you because I needed you
I keep your words in a safe place time can't touch
I've lived long enough to say that finding a friend like you is tough
And now that you're gone I'm left with shadows that dance around me
The one star I had in my darkness was taken; my horizon is empty
Why did you jump?
Why weren't my words there to protect you?
I have failed you as a writer, I have failed you as a friend
It's unfair that I wasn't there for you
It's unfair that your mind told you that jumping was something to do
...
I miss you
...

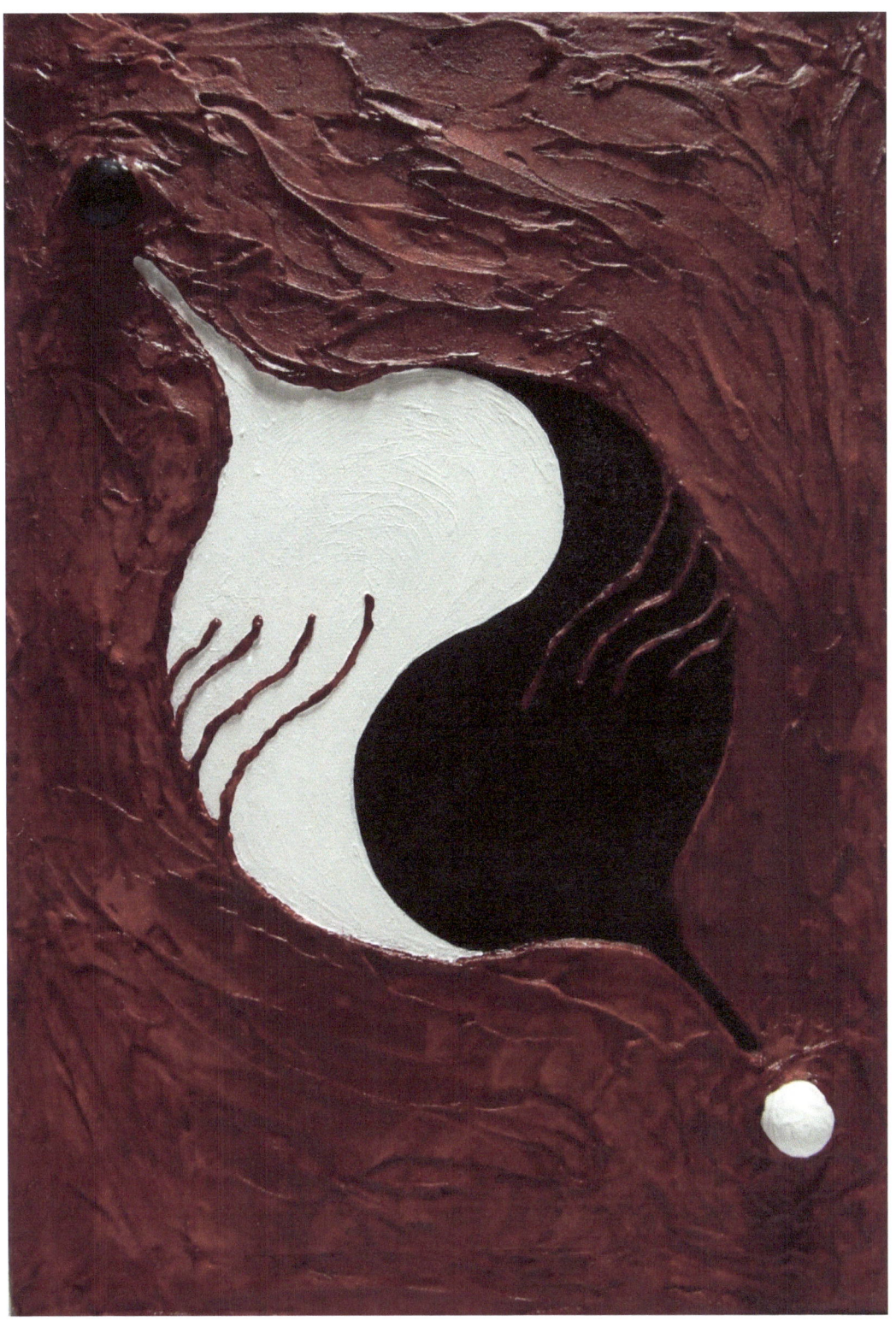

Outro

Breathe
in the fumes that fuel both
the frail and the fighter
stationed to struggle
for freedom from faults
assaulting our frontlines with feral fangs
yet we gamble at this game – crossroads
either take a turn through the thicket where
you'll bleed the truth that'll tarnish your name
or dare to play chess with the devil
who'll deceive you into bedding your shame
whatever you choose there's no retreat
and if you tread past the threshold
the sun and moon will be your halo
for time ticks not for you – you've proven true
or so they say, but I see none who's won
our worth too meagre to pay the fare
past Truth or Dare, and truth be told
this freedom may be a fable
to nudge faint hearts forward
if so, your failures aren't fateful
don't give this bend the title of End.

Chapter 3: Finding Yourself

Intro

Tape my tongue to the fence I straddle
dry with mediocre thoughts
too dull to handle with care or caution
left to flick flies off faecal matter
not that I matter and that is how
the domineering dogs like it
no struggle, stay humble
so there'll be no trouble
step out of their subjugation and
you'll be labelled with a stereotypical definition
that'll be the degradation of your "perfection"
how wrong we are to know what we want
in a place where they hunt
for heathens with an opinion.

FPP

The disgust that arises from this concept is beyond vile
Consuming this revolting construction will taint any future smile
Calling it repulsive would be a compliment
I would get nauseous if it even came close to my lips
Haunted by nightmares were I forced to swallow it
A hideous concept being perpetuated by a gross sense of taste
The ingredients used have been rendered mere waste
It's uncivilized that they have been selling this for a while
It's repugnant and bears a similarity to bile
For who would willingly take a bite of this foul thing?
A vulgar desecration to the inside of this ring
A sickening creation that should never have seen the light of day
A repulsive, abhorrent, simply distasteful way to create dismay
I went to the depths of my creativity
Read every torture method ever used in human history
Spoke to those who have lost the battle for their sanity
But I couldn't find the thought process,
you would have to go through to create this monstrosity
I am lost; what horrible thing did this man go through?
If it were a lady, what did the world ever do to her?
I feel as if this was nothing more than a ghastly tool for revenge
Twisted into a way to alienate your friends
Imagine the tears shed when the lid flips up and its stench starts to sting
To order this atrocious, wicked piece of excrement is close to bullying
...
Pizza is beautiful
The process leading up to its completion is crucial
Why would one taint this sacred dish?
As a pizza lover I have but one wish
Respect pizza
Treat it with care
Don't put things on it that don't belong there
Toppings are there to enhance the taste
Not ruin it because you want to be "creative"
Freedom is for all
But this should be banned all over the world
FPP

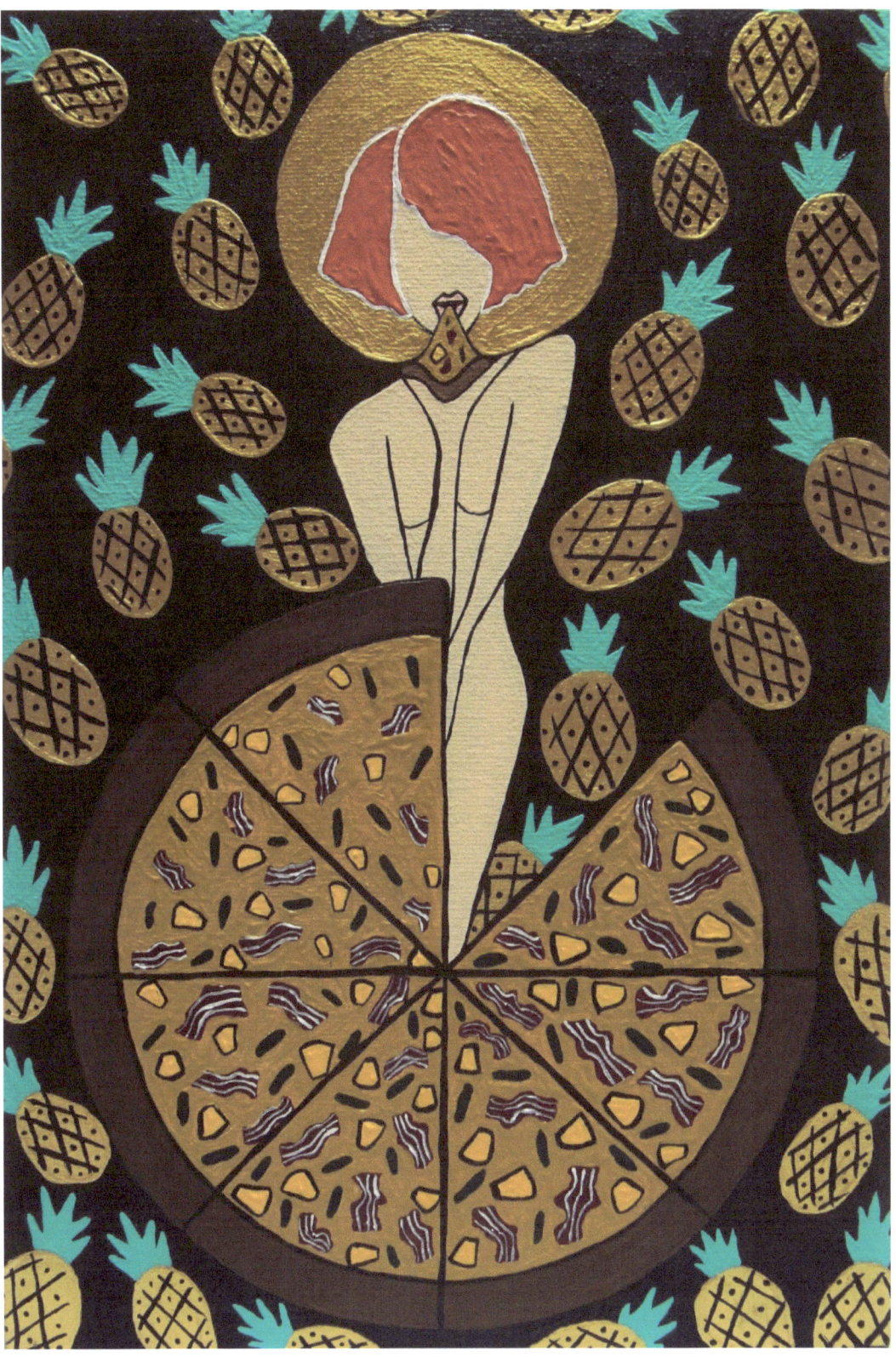

My hair

These dreads are a reflection of my rebellion against the norm
They keep my sanity together when society once again throws me into a storm
Without them I could stand in a culture meant for a select few
Some believe that your hair tells everything about you
The problem is that the story that is being told is often given by the media
Dreads equals weed head even though I don't smoke
Long hair is deemed sexy; that is why fake lines are added
Straight hair is looked at as hot; that's why burning steel touches hair
Curls are enticing; that's why people sleep to twist everything up there
Those tired of the games take a step outside the box and remove it all
Bald or colour it all up, those are the ones who have a ball
Your hair should reflect where you have been and what you've seen
It should be a reflection of your roots and the truth unseen
Your hair should not be destroyed or weakened to satisfy the taste of others
You shouldn't lower or remove anything to please others
A trend isn't reason enough to play with your hair
I would have long since lost myself in the waves of society,
had I listened to my so-called peers
My hair is an extension of my pain, a way to relieve my fears
Let your environment shape your ends
Define reality by using your appearance as the point perception spins around
Let them judge based on things they know nothing of
Beauty isn't in the eye of the beholder
It's inside the person they are looking at
It's time to take your sense of self back
Chisel away the image they told you to be
Find your origin and be your own image of beauty
Play till you find what works
Settle only for what makes you feel good
I won't let it define me, regardless of where society stands
Don't crucify me on your news stands

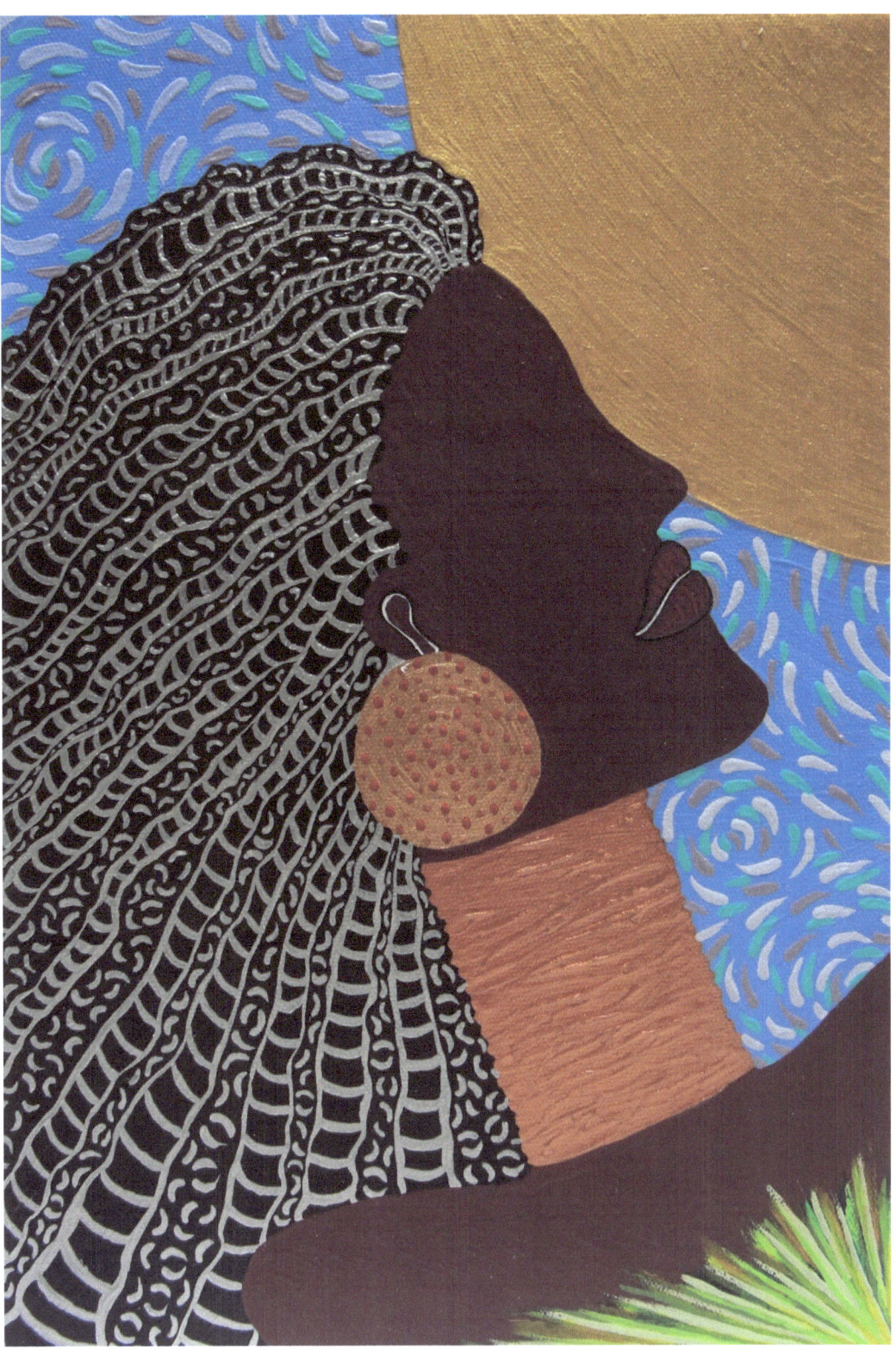

Outro

Losers lost in their losses
that's us, every single being, but
follow the leaders who liken their lack
to a life of learning rather than tally it
to taunt themselves of infected definitions
forged beneath the trivial thunders
of society's scrutinizing claps that clamp
on our fears, festering from being failures
before you cry, chant this truth:
failures are natural
failures aren't final
failures teach us to weave our laurels
failures favour those who wish to find themselves.

Chapter 4: Acceptance

Intro

I rise in the mornings
to meander for meaning
to birth a sense of self
from the www
what would I do without it?
I beg for blue ticks and blushing hearts
whoring for waves of praise
I veil myself with filters
trending tints that titillate
an intangible society
but I am tired, so tired
of styling my form to fit in
a mould not of my making
but mass-produced mimicry.

Im single

People have this idea that you can only be happy in a relationship
As if your life is meant to be spent with somebody else
And if you have failed to find that person, you have failed in life itself
Dismissing the idea of growing on your own and being whole alone
Two parts don't always make one,
and love isn't always eternal even with "the one"
Delusions about relationships solving loneliness are running rampant
People want to have someone around so they don't have to be alone
It has nothing to do with the core values a relationship should be based on
I actually heard someone say, "I'm just with them for this period in my life."
Rendering their partner mere "company" they can leave on a whim
Why are we congratulating people on finding a partner?
As if it is an accomplishment worth praising
As if we are so inherently flawed that finding someone to love us is a feat
We are creating a system where being alone is seen as sad
As if being single is a disease you might want to fix
But what if I don't want company for just this period in my life?
What if I am actually okay with being alone
and don't just want someone around me?
What if I want someone around me who actually adds value to my life?
And people have these fantastic, amazing, miraculous theories about love
How having a partner will help you achieve your dreams,
make you feel better about yourself
Building a future worth living in, making love instead of sex and having
someone there for you
I'm sorry to burst your bubble but all of that just isn't true
Romanticizing love has led to the downfall of many possibly great relationships
People love to think that love will make one stop being human
and remove all flaws
I am single because I have found that people want to be with me for reasons
that have nothing to do with me;
I am sorry but I am not just a cure for feeling lonely
For me a relationship is a commitment
I have found most aren't able to live up to
The previous ones who tried
showed me that love doesn't protect you from reality
And people can still do the most horrible things
and tell you they love you afterwards
I am sorry, but I am single until I can find one
who can convince me they are different
The screening process has proven to be too difficult for some
But I don't care; I would rather stay single and happy
Than be in a relationship just so I have someone waiting for me
Love's meaning has been twisted into having company
I am okay with being single

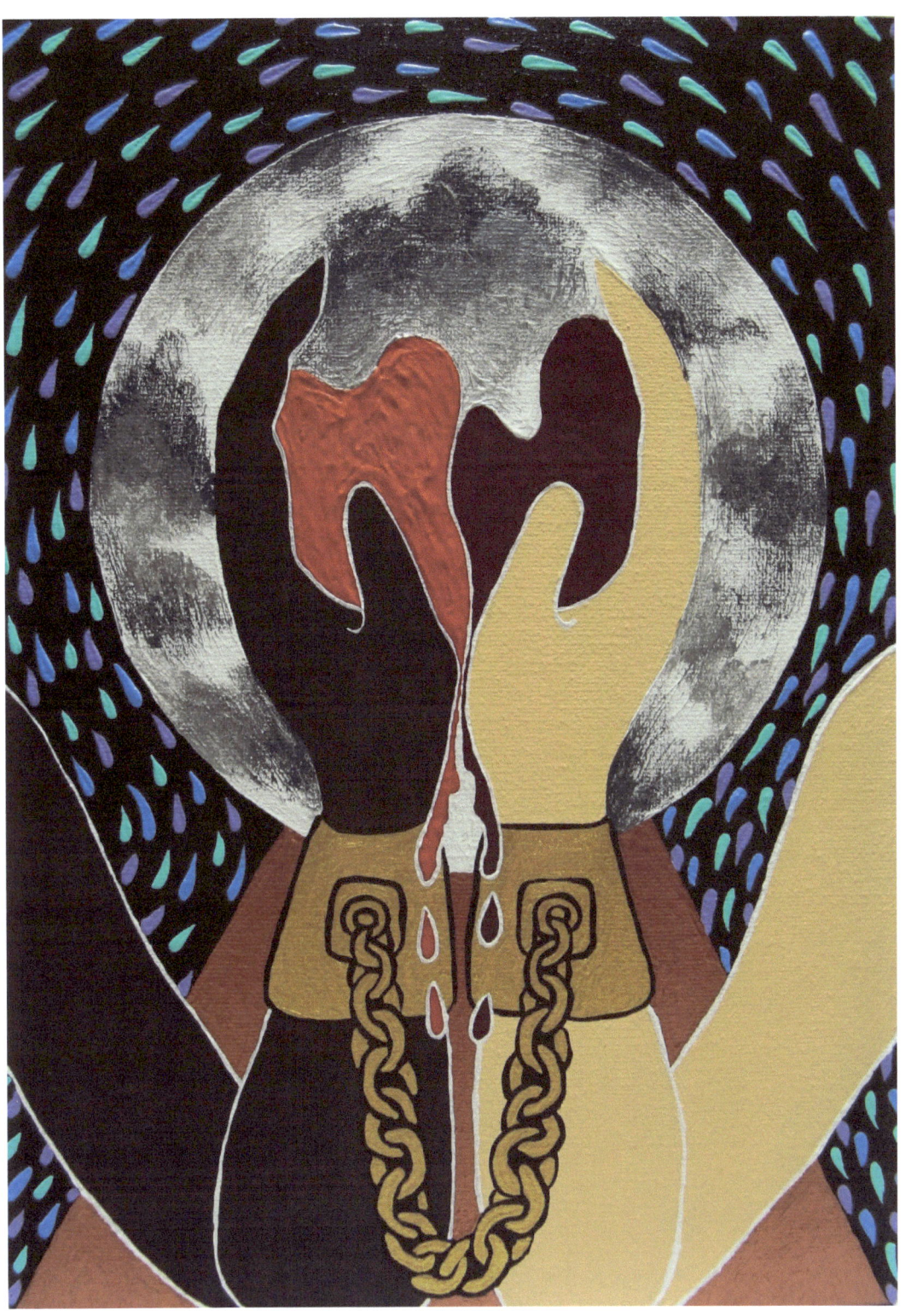

I stink

There he goes, bag over his shoulder as if he is carrying the weight of the world
Contemplating if something this heavy should be bench-pressed or curled
Each step towards this place fills his body with a unique sense of being
As if every muscle in his body knows what he is going to be doing
He stands in front of the door, mentally preparing himself for what's to come
He needs his energy to be up or else none of the exercises can be done

...

Society told him how he needs to look and feel
Society has restricted his perception and convinced him lies are real
Images of a body that is deemed desirable are flung in front of him
Day in and day out, everywhere he goes, a vicious cycle he wears as a ring
Because that's his motivation and drive
A six-pack, arms like steel and a chest that dances as if it were alive

...

He knows it goes step by step, so he takes it one day at a time
Following a regime that he hasn't realized has consumed his mind
His diet keeps him slim and reinforces the idea that he looks good
The fact that he feels dizzy at times
has become a phenomenon that's considered good
Because that means the diet and exercise are working
No pain no gain, drink some supplements and back to running

...

This image of beauty he is chasing is destroying him
To the point where looking sexy is actually an unhealthy thing
Depriving your body of food so you can stay a size you have no business being
Hurting yourself over and over, under the guise that you love exercising
Since when has pain become the way to feel good?
Since when has eating nothing been right?
A car doesn't move because of its body but what's under the hood
And soon your engine will stall, if you keep making its need for gas a fight

...

He stands in front of the mirror in the gym with his shirt off
His muscles flexed, his stomach tightened to seem hard
Both arms up to show his biceps, but still something seems off
For some he has already reached where he needs to be
But all he can see is fat and the parts, which still feel soft
He is lost in a concept given to him by a media that wants to sell products
Spiralling down into a dark place where disorders are the norm
But to him his sweat is the proof that he is doing something worth living for
If he doesn't leave the gym reeking of sweat, he will have to go back in and do more

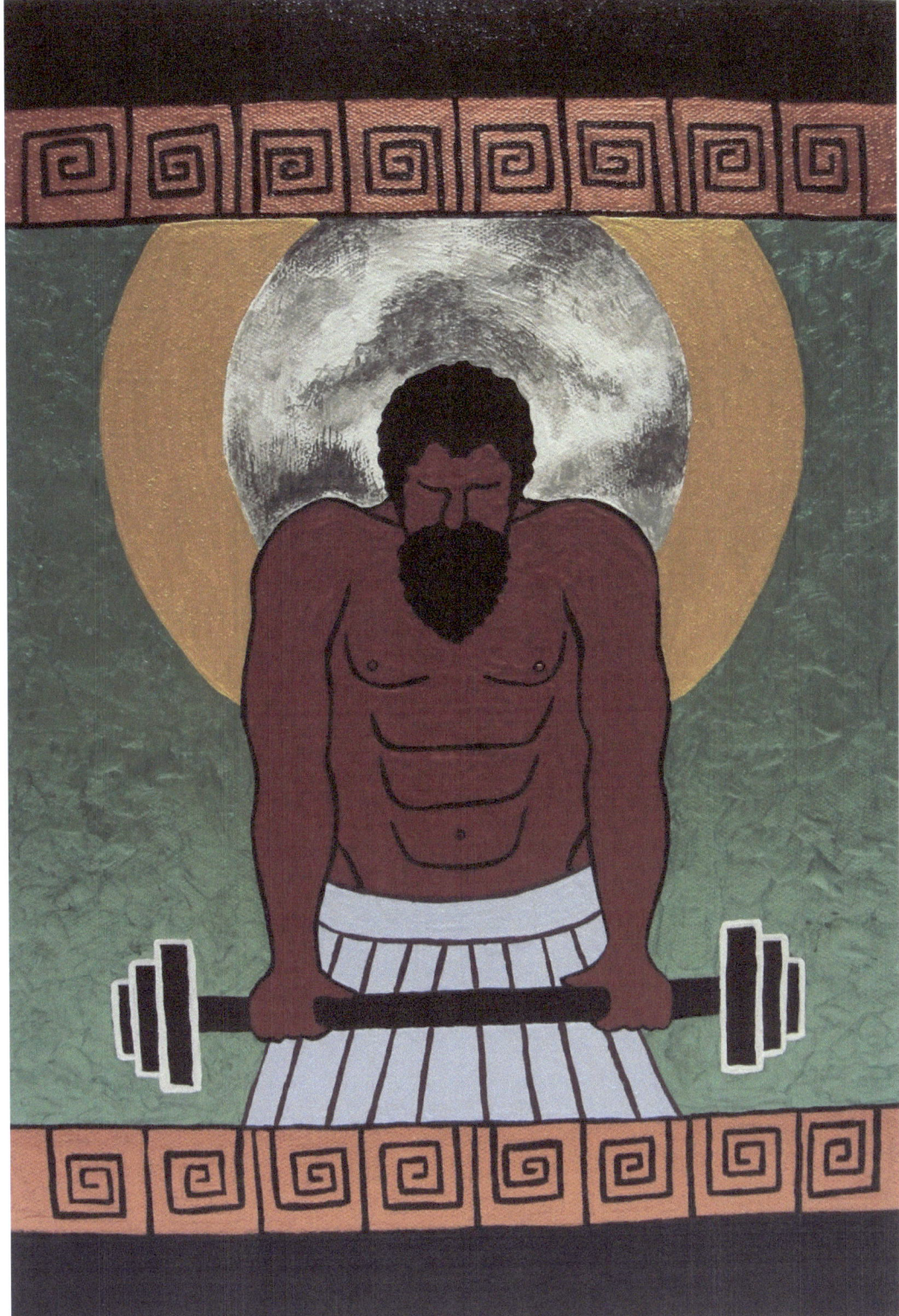

Outro

In darkness I blink
thoughts that slink too fast
for sweaty palms to grasp
they reek of desperation
to embrace my worth
wean off the world
that wakes for menial matters
it will no longer matter to me
my heart and head pound hope
this friction hurts my forlorn frame
but I breathe so this flame may live
warmth only I feel, light only I see
behind flickering eyelids that fan
a spark to fire; I will not retire
till the day this truth transpires.

Chapter 5: Moving On

Intro

As koi dream of donning dragon scales
I dream of morphing into myself
I stand ready to sail into stories
that charts are yet to show
so my grave will be engraved
with words I've come to know
each honest heartbeat hums
the honour of my mission
I'll map out my Atlantis
so break the anchor's bones
and hear the motors moan
no time for tears or fears
this seafarer steers out to see.

Dont listen

Let those tears flow, release them into the world; let your fears go
The wings your future will fly in on are missing more than a few feathers
But perfect is nothing more than an illusion
created by a society trying to hide its own flaws
Run till you feel you can catch the light
that is hiding behind the curtain of insecurity
Appreciate the glass for being there instead of looking to see if it's empty
Let the words slide off your skin and smile as they are flung at you
You decide your worth and you place each step towards your dreams
No one can walk for you or decide your path
See the curves as they come and take it slow
Cry as the sun goes down on dreams you weren't able to uphold through time
Smile at the chances that lie in the possibilities of your yet incomplete mind
Grow into who you feel you need to be
Do what you can and let them call you crazy
Let them tell you that you need to look for comfort
Let them whisper the things that could go wrong, and how you could get hurt
But you, you can abandon your tears onto your cheek
As long as you keep walking on this dusty and empty road
Let those dark clouds sleep in the middle of a sky that's breaking
Know that I am proud of each step you're taking
Know that the future that hides behind that horizon
isn't as scary as they make it out to be
Each small inch you move forward is going towards a down payment
on how you want it to be
Kiss the scars you gain along the way, for they will decorate a beautiful corpse
that lived a life only a few dare dream of
If you fall, grab a hold of the ground,
for it will be there to catch you every single time
Hands to pick you up will not carry that same guarantee
So treat the ground with the same respect it treats you with
For who would love you the same way failing does?
Life is nothing more than an extending moment
in which you are allowed to learn
Learn how to move forward, learn how to appreciate the steps you've taken
Learn how to cry for things you've lost
and smile at things yet to be put on your path
Run where you can run, walk where you can walk
But make sure you never look away from the lines that decorate your road
It's scary, it's terrifying, it's heart-wrenching, it's enough to break your soul
The unknown has always hidden itself behind fear
But you are strong enough to punch through walls
You can ignore those signs of comfort when they start to catcall
I believe in you because you have shown me that you can do it
Drop your tears, throw away your fears, but never let go of yourself
Don't let anyone tell you what you can or can't do

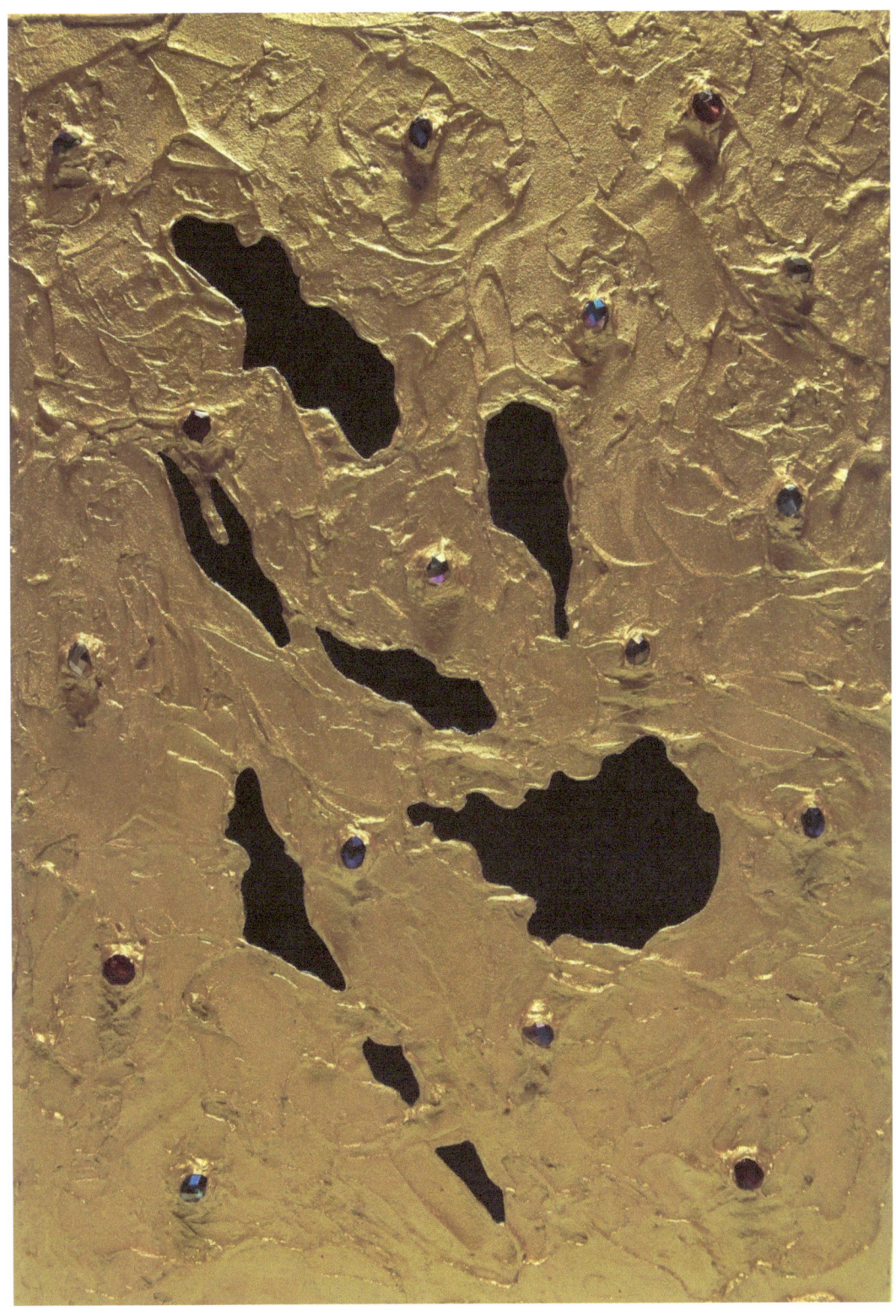

See for yourself

I am in this city where lies have been stacked upon each other
till they reach the sky
The fumes from passing cars must have affected my senses
and rendered me high
Because I swear to you, I can see pigs fly
I came here from this small town called "Other People's Experiences"
The mayor was a nice man called "Prejudices"
Always warned me of the dangers that sleep in the big cities
At times it felt as if he really hated the metropolis called "Possibilities"
But my parents enjoyed having him over for lunch
We always had this dish called "I know better" with a side of "listen to me"
I have always found the aftertaste of those two pretty nasty
After which we would watch their favourite TV show, "Dreams Are for Kids"
I never got that show, but adults really seemed to love it
From time to time we would go shopping on "Comfortable Street"
But you needed this card of "employment" to go into the street
And preferably you would have got your parents' approval to do so
After about twenty years of living there, I figured it was time to go
I got on this train at our only station called "It's Going to Be Scary"
The first stop was "Independence" and at first I was somewhat happy
But then I had to stay there for a while to get a stamp on my ticket
I found out later that only those who travel alone get it
During my time in "Independence" a lot went wrong
I went from sleeping on "Broke Ave" to having dinner
in this cute little diner called "Stay Strong"
But living alone taught me that my "employment" card
wasn't only for "Comfortable Street"
It was to put food on the table and make sure my apartment had heat
But this card required so much time that I was unable to go to the next station
I almost used my "safety" credit card to take a taxi back home
but then I met my friend "Motivation"
He told me that if I stay here too long I will get my "Dreamless" members' card
That was enough for me to move out,
get my stamp and take the train to "It's Going to Be Hard"
But that was just a quick pit stop before reaching "Growing Up"
And now that I'm here, I have to admit that this is my least favourite city
Dishonesty is the language they speak here, manipulation is their currency
"Don't Want to Be Lonely Blvd" seems to be the place to be
But from here I can take this plane to the city called "Possibilities"
I have to deposit my "dreams" and borrow from the "Drive" bank
to pay for the transportation fees
But once I get there, it will all be worth it
Until I can say I live in the city of "Possibilities" my journey can't end
I have to see it for myself

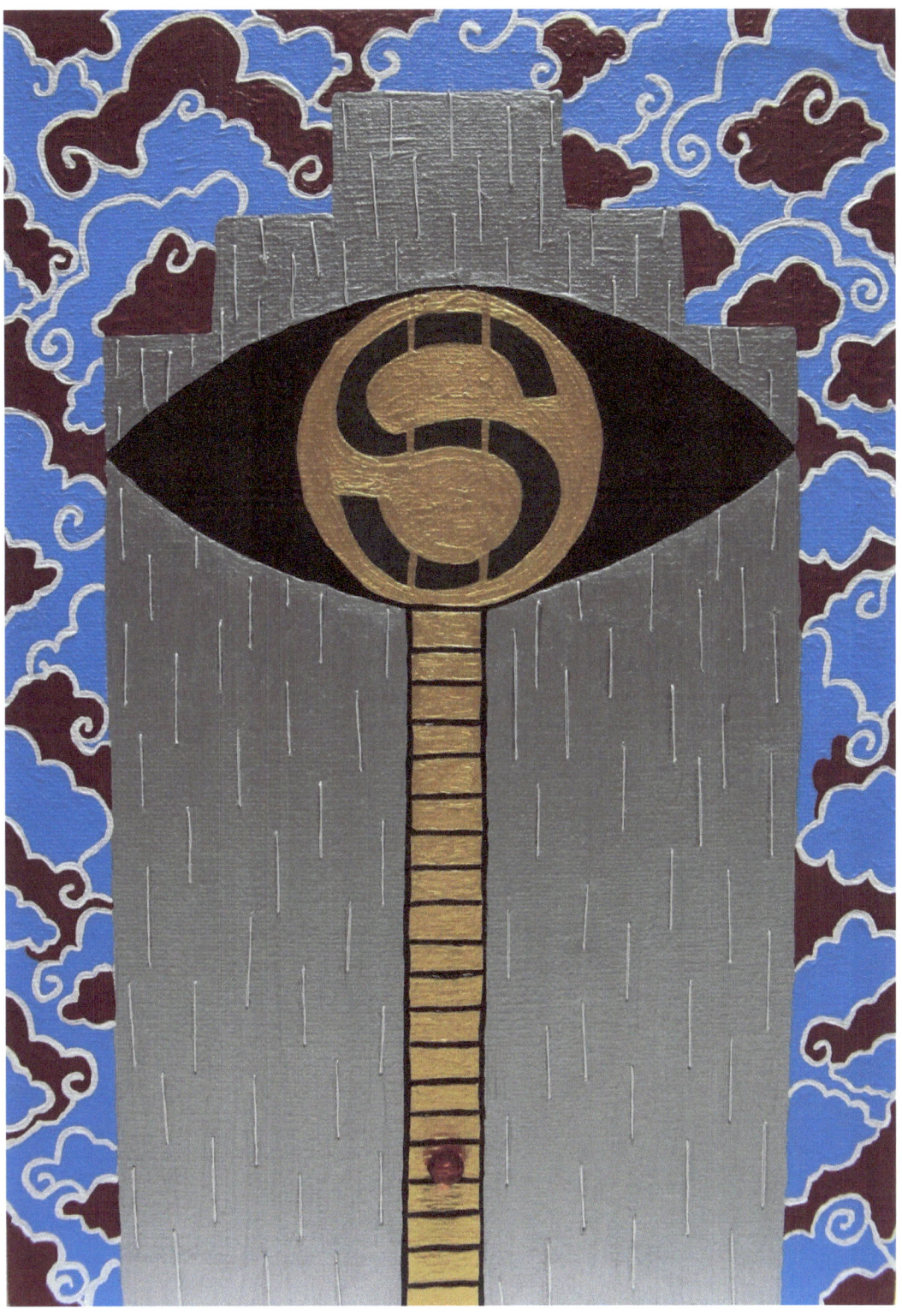

Outro

You've lain in this oasis
shared songs beneath the sky
tasted love from tongue's tip
reminisced on scars still aching
yet found your marbles among the stars
the empire within embraced you
now it is time to see what awaits you...

anntidote.art

Vinovenitas.com

www.ingramcontent.com/pod-product-compliance
Lightning Source LLC
Chambersburg PA
CBHW040411220526
45473CB00004B/1204